HEALTHY DIET AND LIFE STYLE

DR.KHUSHBOO FATIMA

BLUEROSE PUBLISHERS
India | U.K.

Copyright © Dr. Khushboo Fatima 2024

All rights reserved by author. No part of this publication may be reproduced, stored in a retrieval system or transmitted in any form or by any means, electronic, mechanical, photocopying, recording or otherwise, without the prior permission of the author. Although every precaution has been taken to verify the accuracy of the information contained herein, the publisher assumes no responsibility for any errors or omissions. No liability is assumed for damages that may result from the use of information contained within.

BlueRose Publishers takes no responsibility for any damages, losses, or liabilities that may arise from the use or misuse of the information, products, or services provided in this publication.

For permissions requests or inquiries regarding this publication, please contact:

BLUEROSE PUBLISHERS
www.BlueRoseONE.com
info@bluerosepublishers.com
+91 8882 898 898
+4407342408967

ISBN: 978-93-6452-087-4

Cover Design: Shivani
Typesetting: Sagar

First Edition: September 2024

Introduction

"In today's time, when we all are busy and careless about our health, this book is ready to give you a right direction. In this book, we will tell you the importance of a balanced diet and healthy lifestyle. Below you will learn how you can improve your health by making changes in your diet and lifestyle. In this book, we have included topics like diet science, nutrition, exercise, stress management, and soul-care. This book guides you to live a healthy and happy life." - "A new direction for life: with healthy diet and lifestyle.

Contents

Part 1: Foundations of a Healthy Lifestyle 1

  1. Understanding Nutrition: Macronutrients, Micronutrients, and Calorie Needs 2

  2. Setting Health Goals: Assessing Your Current Habits and Setting Realistic Objectives 4

  3. Mindful Eating: Developing a Positive Relationship with Food 7

Part 2: Healthy Eating Habits 9

  1. Foods: Focusing on Fruits, Vegetables, Whole Grains, and Lean Proteins 10

  2. Healthy Hydration: The Importance of Water and Limiting Sugary Drinks 12

Part 3: Lifestyle Habits for Optimal Health 17

  1. Physical Activity: Finding Exercises You Enjoy and Scheduling Them In 18

  2. Stress Management Techniques: Meditation, Yoga, and Deep Breathing 20

  3. Sleep and Relaxation: Prioritizing Restful Nights and Leisure Time 23

  4. Building a Support Network: Surrounding Yourself with Positive Influences 25

Part 4: Managing Chronic Health Conditions* 27

1. Nutrition and Lifestyle Strategies for Managing Diabetes 28

2. Heart-Healthy Habits: Lowering Blood Pressure and Cholesterol 30

3. Gut Health and Immune Function: The Importance of Fiber and Probiotics 33

Part 5: Maintaining a Healthy Lifestyle 37

1. Overcoming Obstacles and Staying Motivated 38

2. Monitoring Progress and Adjusting Your Plan as Needed 40

3. Building Resilience and Practicing Self-Care 42

Appendices 45

1. Healthy Recipes and Meal Plans 46

2. Stress Management Techniques and Mindfulness Exercises 49

3. Workout Routines and Exercise Tips 52

Part 1: Foundations of a Healthy Lifestyle

1.

Understanding Nutrition: Macronutrients, Micronutrients, and Calorie Needs

---

Here's an overview of nutrition basics:

Macronutrients:

1. _Carbohydrates:_ Provide energy, fiber, and nutrients (45-65% of daily calories).
2. _Protein:_ Builds and repairs tissues, organs, and cells (15-20% of daily calories).
3. _Fats:_ Supply energy, absorb vitamins, and maintain cell health (20-35% of daily calories)

Micronutrients:

1. _Vitamins:_ Essential for energy production, immune function, and overall health.

2. _Minerals:_ Crucial for hydration, nerve function, and bone health

Calorie Needs:

1. _Daily caloric intake:_ Varies based on age, gender, weight, height, and activity level.
2. _Basal Metabolic Rate (BMR):_ The number of calories your body needs at rest.
3. _Thermic Effect of Food (TEF):_ The energy expended digesting and processing food.

Tips:

1. _Eat a balanced diet:_ Focus on whole foods, variety, and moderation.
2. _Consult a healthcare professional:_ Determine your individual calorie needs and nutrient requirements
3. _Stay hydrated:_ Drink plenty of water throughout the day.
4. _Be mindful of portion sizes:_ Control the amount of food you eat.
5. _Limit processed and sugary foods:_ Opt for nutrient-dense choices instead.

Remember, understanding nutrition is key to making informed choices about your diet and lifestyle.

2.

Setting Health Goals: Assessing Your Current Habits and Setting Realistic Objectives

Setting health goals involves assessing your current habits and setting realistic objectives. Here's a step-by-step guide:

Assess Your Current Habits:

1. _Track your diet:_ Record your food intake for a week to identify patterns and areas for improvement.
2. _Monitor your physical activity:_ Log your daily activity levels, including exercise and sedentary time.
3. _Evaluate your sleep habits:_ Note your sleep schedule, duration, and quality.
4. _Assess your stress levels:_ Identify sources of stress and coping mechanisms.

Set Realistic Objectives:

1. _Specific:_ Clearly define your goals, such as "I want to lose 10 pounds in 3 months."
2. _Measurable:_ Quantify your goals, like "I will exercise for 30 minutes, 3 times a week."
3. _Achievable:_ Ensure your goals are realistic and attainable based on your lifestyle.
4. _Relevant:_ Align your goals with your values and priorities.
5. _Time-bound:_ Establish a specific timeline for achieving your goals.

Examples of Health Goals:

1. _Nutrition:_ Eat 5 servings of fruits and vegetables daily, reduce sugar intake to 20 grams per day.
2. _Physical Activity:_ Exercise for 30 minutes, 3 times a week, increase daily step count to 10,000 steps.
3. _Sleep:_ Establish a consistent sleep schedule, aim for 7-8 hours of sleep per night.
4. _Stress Management:_ Practice meditation or deep breathing exercises for 10 minutes, 2 times a week.

Remember:

1. _Start small:_ Break down large goals into smaller, manageable steps.
2. _Seek support:_ Share your goals with a friend or family member for accountability.

3. _Be flexible:_ Adjust your goals as needed, and don't be too hard on yourself if you encounter setbacks.
4. _Celebrate progress:_ Acknowledge and celebrate your achievements along the way.

3.

Mindful Eating: Developing a Positive Relationship with Food

Mindful eating involves developing a positive and non-judgmental relationship with food. Here are some tips to cultivate mindful eating:

1. _Pay attention to hunger and fullness cues:_ Eat when hungry, stop when satisfied.
2. _Savor your food:_ Enjoy the flavors, textures, and aromas.
3. _Eat slowly and intentionally:_ Focus on the experience, not just the food.
4. _Eliminate distractions:_ Turn off the TV, put away your phone, and eat in a distraction-free environment.
5. _Practice gratitude:_ Appreciate the food, the people you're with, and the experience.

6. _Develop self-compassion:_ Allow yourself to enjoy food without guilt or shame.
7. _Notice emotions:_ Recognize how emotions influence your eating habits.
8. _Stay present:_ Focus on the present moment, without judgment.

Benefits of mindful eating include:

1. _Improved digestion_
2. _Increased satisfaction_
3. _Healthier relationships with food_
4. _Reduced stress_
5. _Weight management_
6. _Increased self-awareness_

Remember, mindful eating is a journey. Start with small steps, and be patient with yourself as you develop a more positive and intentional relationship with food.

Part 2: Healthy Eating Habits

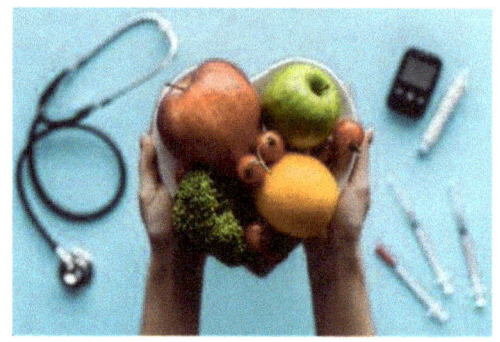

1.

Foods: Focusing on Fruits, Vegetables, Whole Grains, and Lean Proteins

Here are some tips for focusing on whole, nutrient-dense foods:

Fruits:

1. _Aim for variety:_ Include a range of colors to ensure a broad spectrum of nutrients.
2. _Incorporate berries:_ Berries are packed with antioxidants and fiber.
3. _Eat seasonal:_ Enjoy fruits that are in season for optimal flavor and nutrition.

Vegetables:

1. _Dark leafy greens:_ Spinach, kale, and collard greens are rich in vitamins and minerals.

2. _Cruciferous vegetables:_ Broccoli, cauliflower, and Brussels sprouts support cancer prevention.
3. _Colorful vegetables:_ Bell peppers, carrots, and sweet potatoes provide antioxidants and fiber.

Whole Grains:

1. _Choose whole grains:_ Brown rice, quinoa, and whole wheat bread provide fiber and nutrients.
2. _Incorporate legumes:_ Lentils, chickpeas, and black beans are rich in protein and fiber.
3. _Limit refined grains:_ Restrict white bread, sugary snacks, and processed foods.

Lean Proteins:

1. _Include plant-based options:_ Beans, lentils, and tofu are rich in protein and fiber.
2. _Choose lean meats:_ Opt for poultry, fish, and low-fat dairy products.
3. _Limit processed meats:_ Restrict sausages, bacon, and processed snacks.

Remember:

- Focus on whole, unprocessed foods for optimal nutrition.
- Aim for variety and inclusion rather than restriction.
- Consult with a healthcare professional or registered dietitian for personalized guidance.

2.

Healthy Hydration: The Importance of Water and Limiting Sugary Drinks

Here are some tips for healthy hydration:

Importance of Water:

1. _Essential for bodily functions:_ Water is necessary for digestion, circulation, and temperature regulation.

2. _Boosts energy and focus:_ Even mild dehydration can cause fatigue and difficulty concentrating.

3. _Supports weight loss:_ Drinking water can help with appetite control and metabolism.

Limiting Sugary Drinks:

1. _Avoid added sugars:_ Sugary drinks like soda, sports drinks, and sweetened tea/coffee can lead to weight gain and health issues.

2. _Choose water-rich beverages:_ Infused water, seltzer, and unsweetened tea/coffee are healthier alternatives.

3. _Be mindful of portion sizes:_ Even healthy drinks can contribute to excessive calorie intake if consumed in excess.

Tips for Healthy Hydration:

1. _Drink at least 8 cups (64 oz) of water per day:_ Adjust based on individual needs, activity level, and climate.

2. _Monitor urine output:_ Aim for pale yellow or clear urine to ensure proper hydration.

3. _Make water easily accessible:_ Keep a water bottle with you throughout the day.

4. _Infuse water with fruits or herbs:_ Add flavor without added sugars.

5. _Avoid drinking too much water before bed:_ Limit fluids 1-2 hours before bedtime to prevent nighttime awakenings.

Remember, healthy hydration is essential for overall well-being. Make water your go-to beverage and limit sugary drinks to maintain optimal health. 3... Meal Planning and Grocery Shopping Strategies Here are some meal planning and grocery shopping strategies:

Meal Planning:

1. _Plan ahead:_ Create a weekly meal schedule to save time and reduce food waste.

2. _Set a budget:_ Determine how much to spend on groceries and stick to it.

3. _Consider dietary needs:_ Plan meals that accommodate your family's dietary restrictions and preferences.

4. _Keep it simple:_ Choose simple, quick recipes for busy days.

5. _Involve the family:_ Ask for input and ideas from family members.

Grocery Shopping:

1. _Make a list:_ Write down the ingredients needed for your planned meals.

2. _Shop sales:_ Check weekly ads and buy items on sale.

3. _Buy in bulk:_ Purchase non-perishable items in bulk to save money.

4. _Shop the perimeter:_ Focus on whole foods like produce, meats, and dairy.

5. _Avoid impulse buys:_ Stick to your list to avoid unnecessary purchases.

Additional Tips:

1. _Use coupons and cashback apps:_ Take advantage of discounts and rewards.
2. _Shop at local farmers' markets:_ Support local farmers and get fresh produce.
3. _Plan for leftovers:_ Use leftovers to reduce food waste and save time.
4. _Keep a well-stocked pantry:_ Maintain a supply of staples like canned goods, oils, and spices.
5. _Review and adjust:_ Regularly review your meal planning and grocery shopping strategy to make adjustments as needed.

By implementing these strategies, you can save time, money, and reduce stress while ensuring healthy and delicious meals for your family. 4...Cooking Methods and Healthy Recipes Here are some healthy cooking methods and recipes:

Healthy Cooking Methods:

1. _Grilling:_ Retains nutrients and adds smoky flavor.
2. _Roasting:_ Brings out natural sweetness and tenderness.
3. _Steaming:_ Preserves nutrients and delicate flavors.
4. _Stir-frying:_ Quick and easy, with minimal oil.
5. _Baking:_ Low-fat and even cooking.

Healthy Recipes:

1. _Grilled Chicken Salad:_ Mixed greens, grilled chicken, veggies, and citrus vinaigrette.
2. _Roasted Vegetable Soup:_ Seasonal veggies, beans, and whole grains.
3. _Steamed Salmon with Quinoa and Broccoli:_ Lean protein, complex carbs, and steamed veggies.
4. _Stir-Fried Vegetables with Tofu and Brown Rice:_ Plant-based protein, mixed veggies, and whole grains.
5. _Baked Sweet Potato and Black Bean Tacos:_ Complex carbs, plant-based protein, and fiber-rich toppings.

Tips:

1. _Use herbs and spices for flavor:_ Instead of salt and sugar.
2. _Choose lean proteins:_ Poultry, fish, beans, and tofu.
3. _Incorporate healthy fats:_ Nuts, seeds, avocado, and olive oil.
4. _Experiment with new ingredients:_ Try new veggies, whole grains, and legumes.
5. _Keep it simple and fun:_ Cooking should be enjoyable!

Remember, healthy cooking is about balance, variety, and whole foods. Experiment with new recipes and methods to find what works best for you!

Part 3: Lifestyle Habits for Optimal Health

1.

Physical Activity: Finding Exercises You Enjoy and Scheduling Them In

---

Here are some tips for finding exercises you enjoy and scheduling them in:

Finding Exercises You Enjoy:

1. _Explore different activities:_ Try various exercises like walking, running, swimming, cycling, or group fitness classes.

2. _Consider your interests:_ Engage in physical activities related to your hobbies, such as dancing or hiking.

3. _Think about your lifestyle:_ Choose exercises that fit your schedule and preferences, like home workouts or outdoor activities.

4. _Get inspired:_ Follow fitness influencers, read workout blogs, or watch exercise videos.

5. _Consult a professional:_ Talk to a personal trainer or fitness coach to help you find suitable exercises.

Scheduling Exercises:

1. _Create a routine:_ Plan out your workouts for the week, including time and duration.

2. _Start small:_ Begin with manageable sessions (20-30 minutes) and gradually increase duration and frequency.

3. _Schedule it in:_ Treat workouts as non-negotiable appointments and write them in your calendar.

4. _Find a workout buddy:_ Exercise with a friend or family member for motivation and accountability.

5. _Track progress:_ Use a fitness tracker, journal, or mobile app to monitor your progress and stay motivated.

Remember:

- Consistency is key: Aim for regular physical activity, even if it's just a few times a week.

- Listen to your body: Rest when needed, and don't push yourself too hard.

- Make it fun: Enjoy the process, and celebrate small victories along the way!

2.

Stress Management Techniques: Meditation, Yoga, and Deep Breathing

---

Here are some stress management techniques:

Meditation:

1. _Mindfulness meditation:_ Focus on the present moment, without judgment.
2. _Loving-kindness meditation:_ Cultivate kindness and compassion towards yourself and others.
3. _Transcendental meditation:_ Use a mantra to quiet the mind.
4. _Guided meditation:_ Follow a guided audio or visualization.

Yoga:

1. _Hatha yoga:_ Combine physical postures and breathing techniques.

2. _Vinyasa yoga:_ Flow through movements, linking breath and movement.

3. _Restorative yoga:_ Use props to relax and rejuvenate.

4. _Yin yoga:_ Target deep tissue relaxation.

Deep Breathing:

1. _Diaphragmatic breathing:_ Engage the diaphragm, not shallow chest breathing.

2. _4-7-8 breathing:_ Inhale (4), hold (7), exhale (8).

3. _Alternate Nostril Breathing:_ Balance breath and calm the nervous system.

4. _Box Breathing:_ Inhale (4), hold (4), exhale (4), hold (4).

Tips:

1. _Start small:_ Begin with short sessions (5-10 minutes) and gradually increase.

2. _Consistency is key:_ Aim for regular practice, even if it's just a few times a week.

3. _Find what works for you:_ Experiment with different techniques and styles.

4. _Seek guidance:_ Consult with a qualified instructor or healthcare professional.

Remember, stress management is a journey. Be patient, kind, and compassionate with yourself as you explore these techniques.

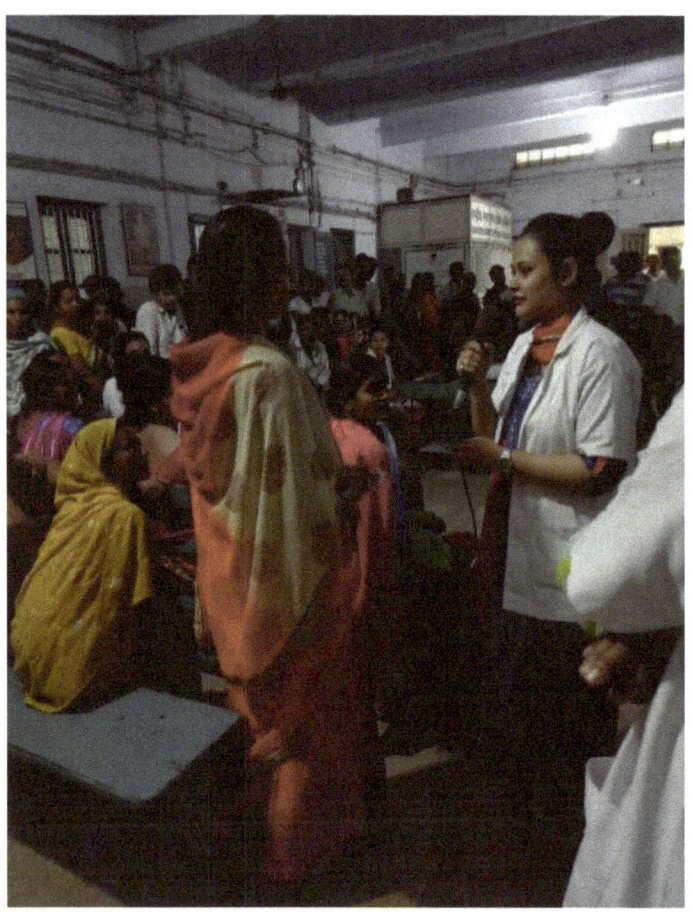

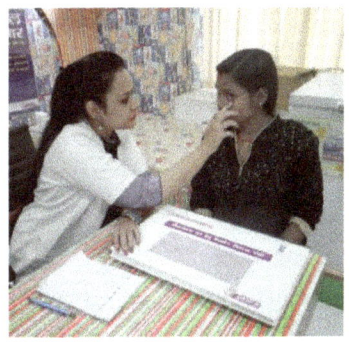

3.

Sleep and Relaxation: Prioritizing Restful Nights and Leisure Time

Here are some tips for prioritizing restful nights and leisure time:

Sleep:

1. _Establish a bedtime routine:_ Wind down with a calming activity, like reading or meditation.
2. _Stick to a sleep schedule:_ Go to bed and wake up at the same time every day.
3. _Create a sleep-conducive environment:_ Make your bedroom dark, quiet, and cool.
4. _Avoid screens before bed:_ The blue light can interfere with your sleep.
5. _Avoid stimulating activities before bed:_ Try to relax and unwind before sleep.

Leisure Time:

1. _Schedule downtime:_ Make time for relaxation and enjoyable activities.

2. _Engage in activities that bring you joy:_ Whether it's reading, listening to music, or spending time with loved ones.

3. _Take breaks throughout the day:_ Take short breaks to stretch, move your body, and rest your mind.

4. _Prioritize self-care:_ Make time for activities that nourish your mind, body, and soul.

5. _Learn to say no:_ Set boundaries and prioritize your own needs.

Remember:

- Adequate sleep and leisure time are essential for physical and mental well-being.

- By prioritizing rest and relaxation, you'll be more productive, focused, and resilient.

- Make time for activities that bring you joy and help you unwind.

4.

Building a Support Network: Surrounding Yourself with Positive Influences

Building a support network is crucial for emotional well-being and resilience. Here are some tips to surround yourself with positive influences:

Identify Positive Influences:

1. _Family and friends:_ Nurture relationships with loved ones who uplift and support you.
2. _Mentors and role models:_ Find individuals who inspire and guide you.
3. _Like-minded communities:_ Join groups or clubs that align with your interests and values.
4. _Support groups:_ Connect with others who share similar challenges or experiences.

Nurture Relationships:

1. _Schedule regular check-ins:_ Stay connected with loved ones and friends.
2. _Show appreciation and gratitude:_ Express thanks and acknowledge support.
3. _Be present and engaged:_ Fully participate in interactions and activities.
4. _Foster open communication:_ Share thoughts, feelings, and concerns openly.

Set Boundaries:

1. _Distance yourself from negativity:_ Limit exposure to toxic individuals or environments.
2. _Establish healthy limits:_ Set clear boundaries to protect time, energy, and emotional well-being.

Cultivate New Connections:

1. _Attend events and gatherings:_ Expand your social circle and meet new people.
2. _Volunteer:_ Engage in activities that bring you joy and help others.
3. _Take classes or workshops:_ Learn new skills and meet like-minded individuals.

Remember:

- Surrounding yourself with positive influences can boost mood, motivation, and resilience.
- Nurture relationships and prioritize connections that uplift and support you.
- Don't be afraid to seek help and expand your support network.

Part 4: Managing Chronic Health Conditions*

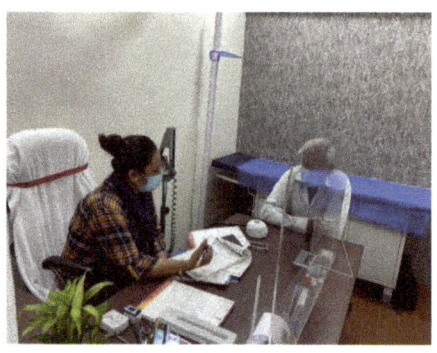

1.

Nutrition and Lifestyle Strategies for Managing Diabetes

Here are some nutrition and lifestyle strategies for managing diabetes:

Nutrition Strategies:

1. _Follow a balanced diet:_ Emphasize whole, unprocessed foods like vegetables, fruits, whole grains, lean proteins, and healthy fats.

2. _Choose complex carbohydrates:_ Focus on whole grains, fruits, and vegetables, which are rich in fiber and nutrients.

3. _Incorporate protein and healthy fats:_ Nuts, seeds, avocado, and olive oil are great sources.

4. _Stay hydrated:_ Drink plenty of water and limit sugary drinks.

5. _Limit added sugars and refined carbohydrates:_ Restrict foods like white bread, sugary snacks, and sweetened beverages.

Lifestyle Strategies:

1. _Regular physical activity:_ Aim for at least 150 minutes of moderate-intensity exercise or 75 minutes of vigorous-intensity exercise per week.
2. _Maintain a healthy weight:_ If overweight or obese, aim for a sustainable weight loss of 0.5-1 kg per week.
3. _Manage stress:_ Engage in stress-reducing activities like yoga, meditation, or deep breathing exercises.
4. _Get enough sleep:_ Aim for 7-8 hours of sleep per night.
5. _Monitor blood glucose levels:_ Regularly check and record your blood glucose levels to understand how different foods and activities affect your levels.

Remember:

- Consult with a certify dietitian or healthcare provider to develop a personalized meal plan.
- Work with your healthcare team to adjust medication and insulin doses as needed.
- Stay informed and up-to-date on the latest diabetes management guidelines and research.

2.

Heart-Healthy Habits: Lowering Blood Pressure and Cholesterol

Here are some heart-healthy habits to help lower blood pressure and cholesterol:

Lowering Blood Pressure:

1. _Exercise regularly:_ Aim for at least 30 minutes of moderate-intensity physical activity most days.
2. _Reduce sodium intake:_ Limit sodium to less than 2,300 milligrams per day.
3. _Increase potassium intake:_ Include potassium-rich foods like bananas, leafy greens, and sweet potatoes.
4. _Stay hydrated:_ Drink plenty of water and limit sugary drinks.
5. _Manage stress:_ Engage in stress-reducing activities like meditation or deep breathing.

Lowering Cholesterol:

1. _Eat a heart-healthy diet:_ Focus on whole grains, fruits, vegetables, lean proteins, and healthy fats.
2. _Increase soluble fiber intake:_ Include foods like oats, barley, nuts, and fruits.
3. _Choose healthy fats:_ Nuts, seeds, avocado, and olive oil are great sources.
4. _Limit dietary cholesterol:_ Restrict foods like egg yolks, organ meats, and high-cholesterol dairy products.
5. _Maintain a healthy weight:_ If overweight or obese, aim for a sustainable weight loss.

Additional Tips:

1. _Get enough sleep:_ Aim for 7-8 hours of sleep per night.
2. _Don't smoke:_ Quitting smoking can significantly lower blood pressure and cholesterol.
3. _Limit alcohol intake:_ Men should limit alcohol to no more than two drinks per day, while women should limit to one drink per day.
4. _Get regular check-ups:_ Monitor blood pressure and cholesterol levels regularly.

Remember to consult with your healthcare provider before making any significant changes to your lifestyle or medication regimen.

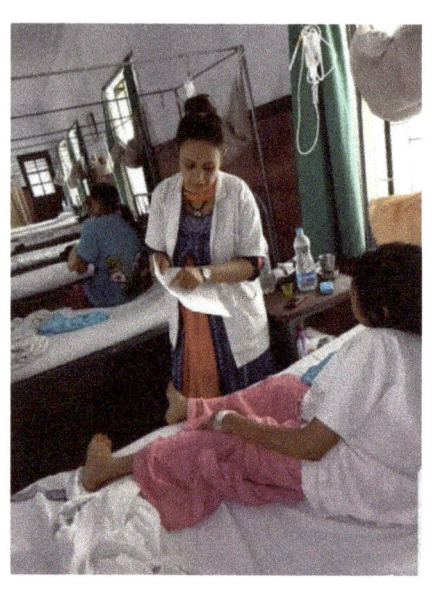

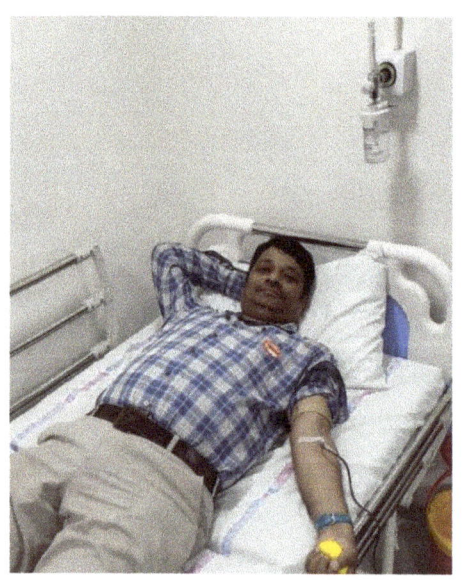

3.

Gut Health and Immune Function: The Importance of Fiber and Probiotics

Gut health and immune function are closely linked, and fiber and probiotics play crucial roles in maintaining a healthy gut and immune system.

Fiber:

1. 1. _Prebiotic properties:_ Fiber feeds good bacteria, promoting their growth and activity.
2. 2. _Gut barrier support:_ Fiber helps maintain the integrity of the gut lining, preventing leaky gut.
3. 3. _Immune system support:_ Fiber helps regulate the immune system, reducing inflammation.

Probiotics:

1. _Beneficial bacteria:_ Probiotics introduce beneficial bacteria into the gut, supporting a balanced microbiome.

2. _Immune system modulation:_ Probiotics interact with the immune system, enhancing its function.

3. _Inflammation reduction:_ Probiotics can reduce inflammation, improving gut health.

Importance of Fiber and Probiotics:

1. _Improved digestion:_ Fiber and probiotics support healthy digestion, reducing symptoms like bloating and constipation.

2. _Boosted immune system:_ A healthy gut microbiome, supported by fiber and probiotics, enhances immune function.

3. _Reduced inflammation:_ Fiber and probiotics can reduce inflammation, lowering the risk of chronic diseases.

4. _Mental health support:_ The gut-brain axis links gut health to mental well-being, with fiber and probiotics playing a role.

Incorporating Fiber and Probiotics:

1. _Eat fiber-rich foods:_ Include fruits, vegetables, whole grains, and legumes in your diet.

2. _Take probiotic supplements:_ Choose a reputable probiotic supplement with multiple strains.

3. _Enjoy fermented foods:_ Include fermented foods like yogurt, kefir, sauerkraut, and kimchi in your diet.

Remember to consult with a healthcare professional before making significant changes to your diet or supplement routine.

Part 5: Maintaining a Healthy Lifestyle

1.

Overcoming Obstacles and Staying Motivated

Here are some tips for overcoming obstacles and staying motivated:

Overcoming Obstacles:

1. _Identify the obstacle:_ Clearly define the challenge you're facing.
2. _Break it down:_ Divide the obstacle into smaller, manageable tasks.
3. _Find a solution:_ Research and explore different solutions.
4. _Seek support:_ Ask for help from friends, family, or professionals.
5. _Take action:_ Start working on the solution.

Staying Motivated:

1. _Set goals:_ Define achievable goals and track progress.
2. _Celebrate milestones:_ Reward yourself for accomplishments.
3. _Find accountability:_ Share goals with a friend or mentor.
4. _Track progress:_ Use a journal or app to monitor progress.
5. _Stay positive:_ Focus on the benefits and positive outcomes.
6. _Be kind to yourself:_ Don't be too hard on yourself when faced with setbacks.
7. _Find inspiration:_ Surround yourself with motivational resources.
8. _Stay consistent:_ Make healthy habits a part of your daily routine.

Remember, overcoming obstacles and staying motivated is a journey. Be patient, stay committed, and celebrate your progress! 2 Monitoring Progress and Adjusting Your Plan as Needed Monitoring progress and adjusting your plan as needed is crucial to achieving your health and wellness goals. Here are some tips to help you do so:

2.

Monitoring Progress and Adjusting Your Plan as Needed

Monitoring Progress:

1. _Track your habits:_ Use a journal, app, or spreadsheet to track your daily habits.

2. _Measure progress:_ Take progress photos, measurements, or track your weight.

3. _Monitor your feelings:_ Pay attention to your energy levels, mood, and overall well-being.

4. _Get feedback:_ Ask for feedback from friends, family, or a healthcare professional.

Adjusting Your Plan:

1. _Identify areas for improvement:_ Analyze your progress and identify areas that need improvement.

2. _Adjust your goals:_ Make adjustments to your goals as needed.
3. _Change your habits:_ Make changes to your daily habits to support your goals.
4. _Seek support:_ Ask for help from friends, family, or a healthcare professional.
5. _Be patient:_ Remember that progress takes time, and be patient with yourself.
6. _Celebrate milestones:_ Celebrate your progress and accomplishments along the way.

Remember, monitoring progress and adjusting your plan is an ongoing process. Stay committed, and don't be afraid to make changes as needed. 3 Building Resilience and Practicing Self-Care Building resilience and practicing self-care are essential for maintaining overall well-being. Here are some tips to help you build resilience and practice self-care:

3.

Building Resilience and Practicing Self-Care

Building Resilience:

1. _Develop a growth mindset:_ View challenges as opportunities for growth.
2. _Practice self-awareness:_ Understand your thoughts, emotions, and behaviors.
3. _Build a support network:_ Surround yourself with positive relationships.
4. _Learn coping skills:_ Develop healthy coping mechanisms, such as mindfulness or journaling.
5. _Take care of your physical health:_ Regular exercise, healthy eating, and sufficient sleep.

Practicing Self-Care:

1. _Prioritize activities that bring joy:_ Make time for hobbies, passions, or creative pursuits.

2. _Practice mindfulness and meditation:_ Regular mindfulness practice can reduce stress and increase calm.
3. _Engage in self-compassion:_ Treat yourself with kindness, understanding, and patience.
4. _Set boundaries:_ Establish healthy limits with others to protect your time and energy.
5. _Take breaks and rest:_ Allow yourself time to relax and recharge.

Remember, building resilience and practicing self-care are ongoing processes. Be patient, kind, and compassionate with yourself as you work to develop these essential skills.

Appendices

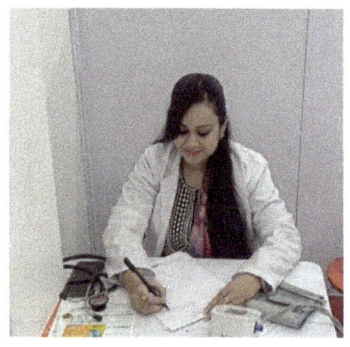

1.

Healthy Recipes and Meal Plans

Here are some healthy recipes and meal plans:

Breakfast Recipes

1. Avocado Toast: Whole-grain bread, mashed avocado, cherry tomatoes, feta cheese.
2. Overnight Oats: Rolled oats, milk, chia seeds, honey, fruits.
3. Greek Yogurt Parfait: Greek yogurt, granola, berries, honey.

Lunch Recipes

1. Grilled Chicken Salad: Mixed greens, grilled chicken, cherry tomatoes, cucumber, balsamic vinaigrette.
2. Whole-Grain Wrap: Whole-grain wrap, hummus, cucumber, tomato, bell peppers.

3. Quinoa Bowl: Cooked quinoa, roasted vegetables, avocado, lemon-tahini dressing.

Dinner Recipes

1. Baked Salmon: Salmon fillet, roasted asparagus, brown rice.
2. Vegetable Stir-Fry: Stir-fried mixed vegetables, brown rice, tofu, soy sauce.
3. Lentil Soup: Red or green lentils, diced vegetables, tomatoes, spinach, olive oil.

Meal Plans

Monday

- Breakfast: Avocado Toast.
- Lunch: Grilled Chicken Salad.
- Dinner: Baked Salmon with Roasted Vegetables.

Tuesday

- Breakfast: Overnight Oats.
- Lunch: Whole-Grain Wrap.
- Dinner: Vegetable Stir-Fry.

Wednesday

- Breakfast: Greek Yogurt Parfait.
- Lunch: Quinoa Bowl.
- Dinner: Lentil Soup.

Thursday

- Breakfast: Smoothie Bowl.
- Lunch: Grilled Chicken Caesar Salad.
- Dinner: Baked Chicken with Roasted Sweet Potatoes.

Friday

- Breakfast: Whole-Grain Waffles with Fresh Fruits
- Lunch: Whole-Grain Pasta with Marinara Sauce and Vegetables.
- Dinner: Grilled Shrimp with Roasted Asparagus and Quinoa.

Remember to stay hydrated by drinking plenty of water throughout the day and adjust the portion sizes and ingredients based on your personal preferences and dietary needs.

2.

Stress Management Techniques and Mindfulness Exercises

Here are some stress management techniques and mindfulness exercises:

Stress Management Techniques:

1. Deep Breathing: Focus on slow, deliberate breaths, inhaling through your nose and exhaling through your mouth.

2. Progressive Muscle Relaxation: Tense and then relax different muscle groups in your body.

3. Exercise: Regular physical activity reduces stress and anxiety.

4. Time Management: Prioritize tasks, set realistic goals, and take breaks.

5. Journaling: Write down your thoughts and feelings to process and release them.

6. Seek Social Support: Connect with friends, family, or a therapist.

7. Get Enough Sleep: Aim for 7-9 hours of restful sleep per night.

8. Healthy Eating: Focus on whole, nutritious foods to support mental well-being.

Mindfulness Exercises:

1. Body Scan: Lie down or sit comfortably, focusing on each body part, releasing any tension.

2. Mindful Walking: Pay attention to your feet touching the ground, the sensation of each step.

3. Loving-Kindness Meditation: Focus on sending kindness to yourself and others.

4. Guided Imagery: Use visualization techniques to create a peaceful, relaxing scene.

5. Mindful Movement: Engage in activities like yoga, tai chi, or qigong with a mindful attitude.

6. Sensory Exploration: Focus on the sights, sounds, smells, tastes, and textures around you.

7. Mantra Repetition: Use a simple phrase or word to calm your mind.

8. Gratitude Practice: Reflect on the things you're thankful for each day.

Remember, everyone is unique, and it's essential to experiment with different techniques to find what works best for you. Start with small, manageable steps, and be patient with yourself as you cultivate stress management and mindfulness skills.

3.

Workout Routines and Exercise Tips

Here's a comprehensive guide to workout routines and exercise tips:

Workout Routines:

1. Cardio: 20-30 minutes, 3-4 times a week (jogging, cycling, swimming).

2. Strength Training: 2-3 times a week (weightlifting, bodyweight exercises).

3. Flexibility: 2-3 times a week (stretching, yoga).

4. High-Intensity Interval Training (HIIT): 2-3 times a week (short bursts of intense exercise).

Exercise Tips:

1. Warm-up: 5-10 minutes before each workout.

2. Start slow: Gradually increase intensity and duration.

3. Focus on form: Proper technique over heavy weights.
4. Listen to your body: Rest when needed, avoid injury.
5. Mix it up: Vary your routine to avoid plateaus.
6. Stay hydrated: Drink plenty of water before, during, and after exercise.
7. Get enough sleep: 7-9 hours for muscle recovery and growth.
8. Make it a habit: Schedule workouts and stick to it.

Additional Tips:

1. Consult a professional: Personal trainer or diet doctor for guidance.
2. Set realistic goals: Achievable milestones for motivation.
3. Track progress: Log workouts, weight, and measurements.
4. Find a workout buddy: Accountability and support.
5. Reward yourself: Celebrate milestones and progress.

Remember, consistency and patience are key. Stick to your workout routine and exercise tips, and you'll see progress over time!

www.ingramcontent.com/pod-product-compliance
Lightning Source LLC
LaVergne TN
LVHW061626070526
838199LV00070B/6597